JAKE'S DOOR

JAKE HAMILTON

Snappy Dog
PRODUCTIONS
DENVER, COLORADO

To Dad:
My editor, encourager, and best friend.

A very special thank you to Tamara Dever at TLC Book Design.
Without your amazing talent, expert guidance and infinite patience,
there's no way this book would have come together like it did. You're the best!

JAKE'S DOOR
Copyright © 2020 by Jake Hamilton

Published by Snappy Dog Productions
PO Box 630966 | Littleton, CO 80163

Cover and interior design: TLC Book Design, TLCBookDesign.com

CLAIM YOUR READERS ONLY BONUS HERE! JakesDoor.com/readers

Paperback ISBN: 978-0-9800589-1-8
Ebook ISBN: 978-0-9800589-2-5

First Edition

LCCN: 2020921635

FOREWORD

Like clockwork, it happens every night.

I (Jake's Dad) will be sitting on the sofa, or in my office, or laying in bed. Suddenly Jake shows up beside me, a big smile on his face and his white board in his hand. He's drawn another comic, and he's ready to share it.

While I look it over, Jake studies my face for genuine laughter (often the case) and is always eager for my feedback: "Anything I should change? On a scale of 1–10, how much do you think people will like it?" After we agree on some final tweaks, he snaps a picture with my phone and we post it to his online accounts.

Then it's off to bed for him while I read the comments that roll in from his fans all around the world.

Sure, as a responsible father I probably ought to reinforce how much teenagers need their sleep, and all the reasons we shouldn't make this into a habit on school nights. But the truth is, I cherish the connection I have with my son; how his God-given talent and humor have brought us closer through this journey. I get a genuine thrill when he shows up with that excited smile and fresh whiteboard comic. It's the best part of my night!

As his comic portfolio (and his online following) continue to grow, the most frequently asked question we receive seems to be: "Where do these ideas come from?"

My typical response is that I have no idea—like an endless spring, they just keep bubbling up into his mind, then into his sketchbook, then onto his white board. However, looking back over Jake's life, there certainly are clues.

Jake has always been a keen observer. He studies people, the world around him, and any book he can get his hands on—then somehow these reflections make their way into his comics. He was seven when I first noticed how sharp his eyes were. I was flipping through one of his sketchbooks, and came across a random chart he had drawn about our family's habits. While I had no idea he was studying us, I was forced to admit it was devastatingly accurate.

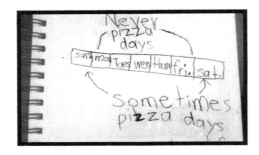

In addition, Jake has an astounding sense of empathy. Perhaps the true nature of any artist is their ability to draw out and connect with the thoughts and feelings of their audience; it's how they can entertain and inspire us. As a big brother, I've seen Jake apply this level of caring and connection to his siblings. In fact, when asked what he wants to be when he grows up, Jake gives the prompt answer of a kid who has given it some serious thought:

"A comic artist, a video game designer, or a doctor to cure my sister's Type 1 Diabetes."

That always moves me. And if he does decide to go the medical route, I'm going to include something with his med school application: this drawing he made in second grade, when a teacher asked him to draw what he imagined the inside of our bodies looks like. I really think Jake nailed it.

Like every parent worth their salt, Jake's mom and I want our kids to go bigger, farther, and have more success than anything we've ever accomplished. The fact that you're reading this foreword in a book Jake is publishing at the age of 14 means he is already surpassing his old man. I couldn't be more pleased, not just with what he has achieved, but also with the attitude and heart with which he's achieving it.

Jake, I'm so proud of you, son! I hope you continue to use your gifts to bring laughter and light into people's lives. It's just one of the many ways you're going to change the world.

Love, Dad

by Jake, age 4

Experimenting with more efficient methods of reaching space, NASA introduces the Giraffe-Forklift Program.

Now that the kids knew his secrets, Santa couldn't let them escape.

THE DAILY STUFF
Man Arrested For Everything
AIL
"We don't know how he did it," say officials
God interviewed, "I have no idea"
Jake Hamilton

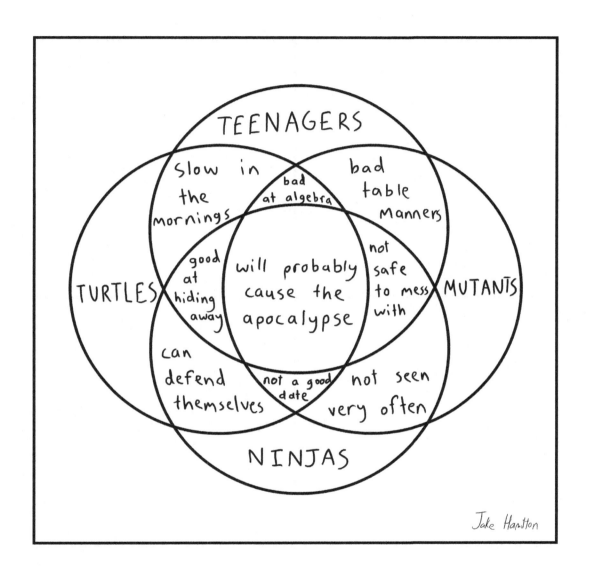

DID YOU KNOW...

8 out of every
10 PEOPLE...

-[MAKE UP]--------

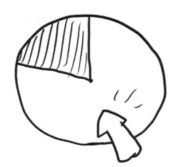

80% of the world's population ???

Jake Hamilton

NEW: apple iApple

sleek.
Modern.
innovative.

Jake Hanton

REVIEWS:

⭐

-microsoft

"You have hit a new low, Apple."

⭐⭐⭐⭐⭐

-anonymous

"yummy on my salad"

In other news, at the biggest pumpkin competition at the halloween festival, the winner was disqualified after judges found out that the pumpkin was not a pumpkin, but in fact a tree with a sign on it.
this is a pumpkin
Jake Hamilton

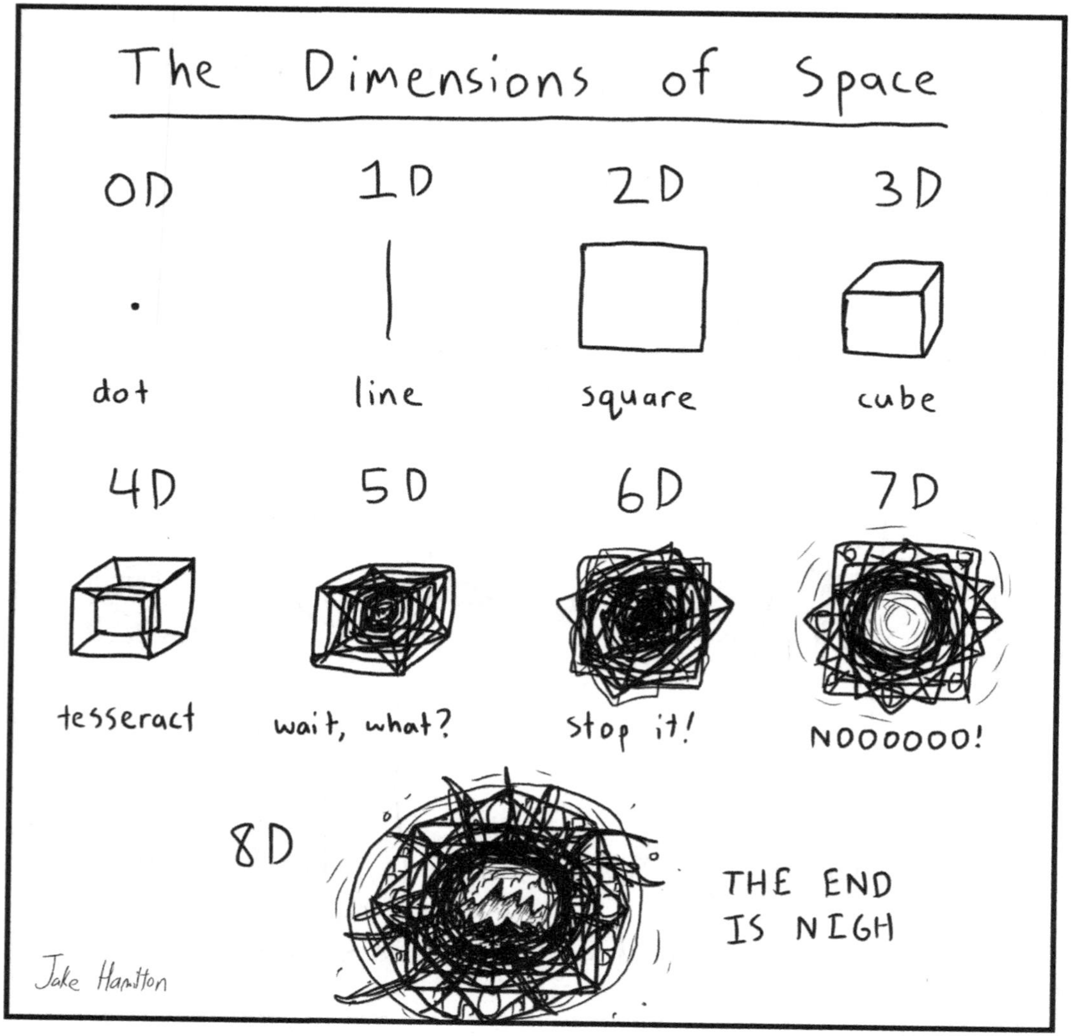
The Dimensions of Space
0D
1D
2D
3D
dot
line
square
cube
4D
5D
6D
7D
tesseract
wait, what?
stop it!
NOOOOOO!
8D
THE END
IS NIGH
Jake Hamilton

THE DAILY STUFF
Large rabbit caught tresspassing
JAIL
"It was just for the kids," possible kidnapping scheme
drugs!!??!!?!?!?
Bomb squad to investigate orb-shaped objects
Jake Hamilton

HOROSCOPES

Aquarius: These horoscopes are 100% accurate.

Pisces: The FISH will protect you.

Aries: Nothing can go badly when you're in a huge hampster ball.

Taurus: Don't cry over spilled milk. Do cry over spilled soda, though.

Gemini: I dunno. Go ask a fortune cookie.

Cancer: The name says it all.

Leo: Yellow snow will be your nemesis today.

Virgo: Look out for falling anvils.

Libra: You will die! Not today, but someday.

Scorpio: You are drooling. Stop.

Sagittarius: You could shut up a LOT more.

Capricorn: There's a mysterious, bright, yellow orb in the sky that's not letting us see the stars, so no luck.

Jake Hamilton

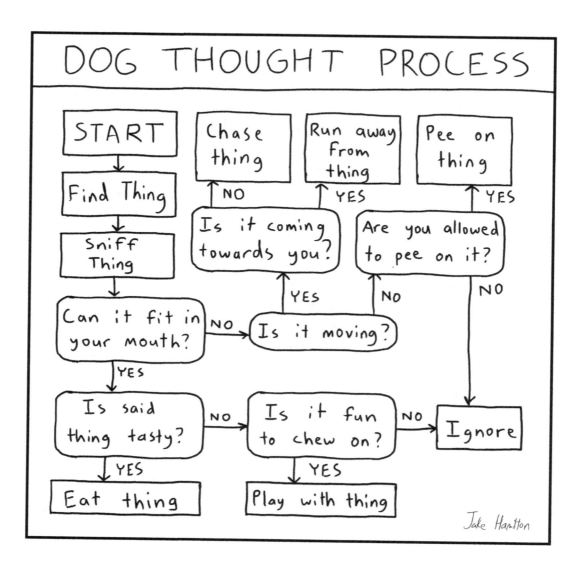

want some ice cream?
nah, I lack toes in taller ants!
don't you mean lactose intolerant?
no, my tall ant has no toes!
help I can't stand
Jake Hamilton

Little did Stan know that he had missed a very important memo.

It was at that moment that Joe got the idea for a more efficient way to wash his chickens.
BAWK
BAWK
BAWK
Jake Hamilton

THE DAILY STUFF
Mysterious man kidnaps hundreds of children!
POLAR EXPRESS
Hundreds gone
Investigation underway
Jake Hamilton

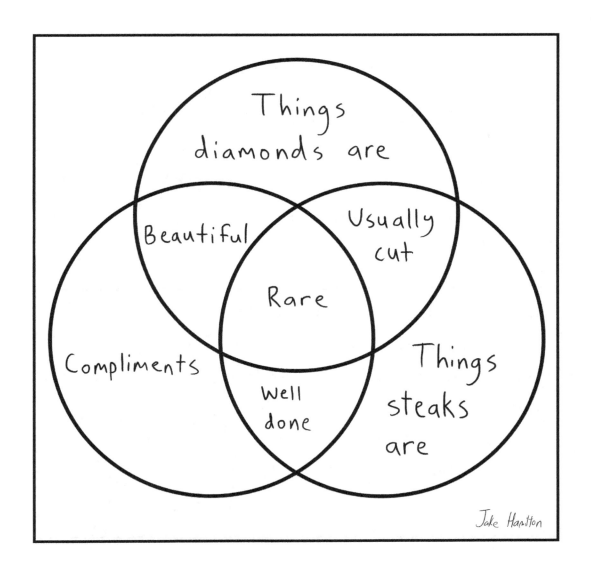

After the Big Bang, dust was scattered all across the universe, which gravity condensed into stars. Some of the dust condensed into planet-
You're supposed to be explaining to me why you stole all my money and spent it on your video game.
I'm getting there!
Jake Hamilton

Babe Ruth saves the dinos

Good night sweetie, and don't let the bedbugs bite!
Or the bedrats. Or the bedsnakes. Or the bedspiders.
Oh, and especially not the bedwolf.
what's a bedwo-
AAAAAAAAAA
Jake Hamilton

APPENDIX

Just like your appendix, it's not clear what purpose or value this section has; also, it could explode at any moment. But Jake has given me permission to add any interesting anecdotes or backstory to his comics here! – Dave (Jake's Dad)

Numbers refer to the comic's page number.

1 Wrong Side of the Bed A good friend of the family named Mike, who is living abroad, follows Jake's comics online and constantly encourages him. One day Mike challenged Jake with a writing prompt: "Can Jake draw a comic based on the phrase 'waking up on the wrong side of the bed'?"

Jake accepted the challenge and the next morning this was drawn on his whiteboard. I posted it to Reddit after he went to school; by the time he got home, the post had over 40,000 upvotes. Thanks for the nudge, Mike!

2 Lightbulb This was ground zero—the very first comic that started Jake's online popularity. For a while, his mom and I were simply posting his comics to our personal Facebook accounts—and getting 20 likes was a pretty big deal. This one got over 60,000 upvotes on Reddit. Jake became a celebrity in eighth grade. Even teachers told him they were fans. Flattering, but for a guy like Jake, uncomfortable. It didn't help when I told him "you've got more fans than would

fit in an NFL stadium!" This really blew his circuits. He and I had a heart-to-heart about whether we should continue this endeavor—if it affected his heart in a negative way, we would shut the whole thing down. After some thought, he decided that if his art could make people smile, and brighten their day a bit, then it was worth it. Proud of this kid.

7 Hormones The start of Jake's comic career coincided with his introduction to puberty. As the great philosopher Ice Cube once said, "Our art is a reflection of our reality."

9 Sploosh Definitely one of my favorites. This comic shows a subtle, yet complex humor that had me reading it a few times before really appreciating it. To convey that it's the same guy in every panel, Jake needed to make him unique, so he gave him a bowler hat. Very dapper.

10 Zombie I have always appreciated a good zombie story. But it took Jake to teach me to have compassion for them.

11 Pencil This was the first comic where Jake's fans recognized his "dark side." I personally think this guy had it coming.

13 Claustrophobia Did you know that on the site Reddit, there is a private group (subreddit) called r/AAAAAAAAAAAAAAAA that has over 285,000 members? Neither did we. But Jake was warmly embraced as one of their own when he posted this one.

14 Proton Pack I'm always so proud when Jake mixes '80s references into his comics. And the science checks out on this genie strategy, I think it just might work!

19 Profits Interestingly, Jake got some pushback from this comic. Specifically, how does a 14-year-old kid know office culture so well? His simple answer—he reads Dilbert. Thanks, Mr. Scott Adams!

20 Fourth Wall This is a great comic, but it some fans commented with the most common critique Jake receives: "There's no way a 14-year-old kid drew this. Must be his dad drawing these and trying to capitalize on his kid." The comments usually contain more colorful language, but these accusations typically make Jake smile. Since it really is him creating the comics (and since his dad isn't nearly that clever) it comes off as a great compliment. But to respond to these critics, I actually filmed Jake drawing a comic in real time. You can watch the video on his Instagram page.

25 Cookie Loaf I distinctly remember riding in the car with Jake, and him asking how normal bread got "puffy" while pita bread did not. I told him about yeast, and then he got silent, pondering the possibilities. This comic came a few hours later.

27 Lemonade Stand In the midst of a pandemic where unemployment rates were soaring, I think this hit a bit close to home with some of his fans. Also, Jake is really good at drawing a guy sweating. Am I right?

29 Sir Carl This comic spurred a lively (albeit gross) online discussion about bathroom practices in medieval times.

A Redditor called u/andybrick95 contributed to this comment:

"Historically, knights would just go and do their duty in their armor while they were doing their duty on the battlefield. It was the job of the knaves to help them out of the armor and clean up all the blood and other bodily substances that ended up on the armor, inside and out. Life in the pre-modern-toilet era is really interesting to look at; dealing with human waste was a huge factor in tons of stuff. For example, castle moats weren't for alligators or sharks; they were cesspools that would hold the people's waste. Often times the walls would have to be built higher as the years went on, or else invaders could simply climb up the piles of excrement to get over the walls. Source: *Poop Happened!: A History of the World from the Bottom Up* by Sarah Albee."

Inspired by this insightful poop comment, Jake responded with this custom comic, and dedicated it to u/andybrick95.

31 Chicken Road Research One of Jake's first Easter eggs in a comic. Totally his idea. Did you see it?

34 Wallet I'm still pondering the ethics of this one.

35 Detective We started watching an awesome British show called "Sherlock." It was just a matter of time before a relevant comic appeared.

36 We've Got Humans A Redditor commenting on this comic gave Jake perhaps the greatest compliment of his young career: "I'm getting a serious Far Side vibe from this

one." To be compared to the master (Gary Larson) is high praise indeed!

37 Hammerhead Jake and I had a great conversation and a good laugh about the likelihood a beach would have a sign that simply says "Beach." But he's right, it works.

39 Apple iApple I would like to point out that Jake uses an iPhone and drew the final version of this comic on a Macbook Pro. As a favor, I would like to personally request that Mr. Tim Cook not sue Jake over this comic. Just having fun (nervous laughter), right?

45 Candy Hearts Not sure, but this may hinder Jake's prospects for a future girlfriend.

47 Captain Obvious The guy on the screen was absolutely inspired by Major Monogram. Jake's contemporaries will understand.

59 Gas Sprinkler Again, the dark side of Jake comes out. What would the next panel show?

60 General's Therapy Some fans appreciated that Jake got the DEFCON level correct; "1" is the worst. Not a coincidence that we watched "War Games" shortly before this comic was drawn.

65 Homonym Tim All grammar aside, I think this is a really well drawn forest and stream!

66 Dog Thought Process Jake's dog Cooper has verified this flowchart many times over.

68 Is Your Fridge Running Jake's generation has never known a world without caller ID, so he missed out on a lot of awesome prank calling. But I'm glad he can appreciate the classics.

70 Lamp This is one of the many comics about dad jokes, with which I frequently bombard Jake. Not sure if there's a message in here for me.

79 Big Fan Jake drew this one in 2020, an election year. Many fans have drawn parallels to a particular candidate, but I need to steal a line from Hollywood films: "Any resemblance to actual persons—living or dead—is purely coincidental."

82 Poop Con Growing up, my mom (Jake's grandmother) had a big problem with "bathroom jokes." Unfortunately, it didn't deter the frequent giggling over poop jokes, and looks like this trend has continued with Jake. Sorry, Mom, this one is kind of funny. :D

86 Santa's First Day So this is what Santa looked like early in his career. And were there really chimneys in stables?

89 Square The response from Jake's introvert fans showed he really nailed this one.

90 The Game I strongly encouraged Jake not to post this one. "No one will get it," I told him, "I sure don't." I was wrong. A LOT of people know about "THE GAME."

According to Wikipedia, these are the widely regarded rules to The Game:

1. Everyone in the world is playing The Game. A person cannot refuse to play The Game; it does not require consent to play and one can never stop playing.

2. Whenever one thinks about The Game, one loses.

3. Losses must be announced. This can be verbally, with a phrase such as "I just lost The Game", or in any other way: for example, via Facebook.

P.S. If you're reading this, you just lost The Game.

91 Updog I introduced Jake to one of my favorite TV shows, "The Office." This comic was drawn the day after we watched Michael Scott learn the updog joke from Jim. Google "office updog" and you'll see what I mean.

97 DIY I don't know what to say about this one, other than this recurring character's name is Chromble (pronounced KROM-bul).

98 Duck Sauce Full disclosure, this one was my idea. I love duck sauce when we eat at Chinese restaurants, but I always imagine them squeezing ducks and packaging the goo that comes out. I really should let the expert handle the humor, I know.

100 Latin Jake really liked his Latin class, and that had a lot to do with his amazing teacher, Mr. Levin. This comic is a tribute to him—the tie, beard, and man bun were spot on. Thanks Mr. Levin!

102 **Billion-Sided Die** I don't know if Jake's generation gets into Dungeons and Dragons as much as mine did, but my D&D buddies and I appreciate the reference. Or is he making fun of us?

110 **Joseph Mother** The prevalence of "Joe Mama" jokes in our family can be traced back to watching the movie "Remember the Titans." But apparently, these jokes were common in medieval times as well.

111 **Minesweeper** Jake got pretty obsessed with this classic Windows game. Regarding this president resembling any current or past president, please see the disclaimer on "Big Fan" above.

115 **Rickroll** Mr. Rick Astley, if you're reading this, you're an inspiration to us all!

ABOUT JAKE

JAKE HAMILTON is an ordinary 14 year old kid with an extraordinary ability to make people laugh through his unique style of comics drawn on his bedroom door whiteboard.

Armed with an insightful wit, a dry erase marker, and a heart of gold, Jake has inspired thousands of worldwide fans who eagerly await his weekly "door comics" online postings.

When not creating, Jake can be found riding bikes, practicing Tae Kwon Do, and playing with his little dog Cooper.

FOR A SPECIAL READERS-ONLY BONUS, VISIT: WWW.JAKESDOOR.COM/BONUS

Made in the USA
Middletown, DE
13 December 2020